Famous Friends:

Babe Ruth
AND
Lou Gehrig

*How They Met, Their Humble Beginnings
and Amazing Achievements*

Michael DeMocker

CURIOUS
FOX
BOOKS

ABOUT THE AUTHOR: While Michael DeMocker has written numerous books for young readers, his main job is as a photojournalist in New Orleans. He was born in the backseat of his dad's car in the parking lot of the local AAA baseball team's stadium in Rochester, New York. He grew up loving baseball, had a Cincinnati Reds hat he didn't remove for years, and batted .467 his senior year in high school while playing first base.

© 2024 by Curious Fox Books™, an imprint of Fox Chapel Publishing Company, Inc., 903 Square Street, Mount Joy, PA 17552.

Famous Friends: Babe Ruth and Lou Gehrig is a revision of *Famous Friends: True Tales of Friendship: Babe Ruth and Lou Gehrig*, published in 2020 by Purple Toad Publishing, Inc. Reproduction of its contents is strictly prohibited without written permission from the rights holder.

PUBLISHER'S NOTE: This story has not been authorized by the estates of Babe Ruth or Lou Gehrig.

Paperback ISBN 979-8-89094-008-7
Hardcover ISBN 979-8-89094-009-4

Library of Congress Control Number: 2023952475

To learn more about the other great books from Fox Chapel Publishing, or to find a retailer near you, call toll-free 800-457-9112 or visit us at *www.FoxChapelPublishing.com*.

We are always looking for talented authors. To submit an idea, please send a brief inquiry to acquisitions@foxchapelpublishing.com.

Fox Chapel Publishing makes every effort to use environmentally friendly paper for printing.

Printed in China

CONTENTS

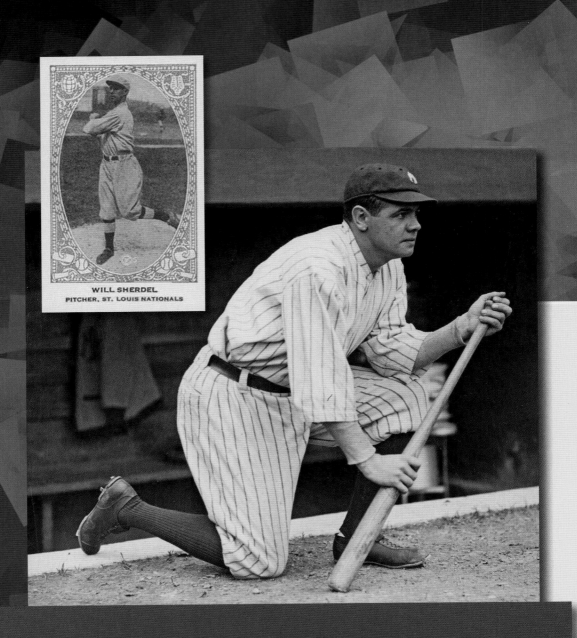

WILL SHERDEL
PITCHER, ST. LOUIS NATIONALS

St. Louis Cardinals pitcher Bill Sherdel (top) faced Babe Ruth in the fourth and final game of the 1928 World Series. Ruth hit three home runs, two off Sherdel, to give the Yankees a World Series sweep.

World Series Heroes

The man stepped into the batter's box, eyeing the pitcher. The fans of the hometown St. Louis Cardinals craned their necks in anticipation. Their team was already behind three games to none to the mighty New York Yankees in this World Series, but the Cardinals had battled throughout the game, clinging to a 2-1 lead in the top of the seventh inning. The man at the plate, already a legend, had seen his championship dreams dashed by this same St. Louis Cardinals team two years before. The Cardinals beat him and his Yankees in seven games in the 1926 World Series. Despite playing on an injured ankle, Babe Ruth was going to make sure that didn't happen again in 1928.

Cardinals pitcher Bill Sherdel got ahead of Ruth in the count, throwing two strikes. One more good pitch and the "Sultan of Swat" would have to take the long walk back to the dugout. The pitcher wound up and threw. Ruth swung and the crack of the bat was heard by every one of the 37,331 fans inside Sportsman's Park. The ball sailed high and deep over the right field fence for a home run to tie the game. Ruth rounded the bases and was greeted by his friend and teammate Lou Gehrig, who congratulated him on his monster home run.

Lou Gehrig in 1923 during his rookie year with the New York Yankees.

Now, it was Gehrig's turn to bat. The game was tied, so the Cardinals still had a chance to pull this one out and continue the series. Bill Sherdel also got two strikes on Gehrig, putting the young Yankees slugger on the verge of striking out. But, like his friend and mentor Ruth, he hit the two-strike pitch deep over the right field wall, giving the Yankees a lead they would never give up. When the game was finally over, Ruth had hit three home runs, tying his own record for home runs in a World Series game. Gehrig finished the four-game series with a .545 batting average and four home runs. He also drove in as many runs as the entire St. Louis team combined! The Yankees became the first team in history to sweep back-to-back championships.

New York Yankees teammates Babe Ruth and Lou Gehrig could not have been more different, personality-wise. The older Ruth was brash and loud, a party animal, and a nearly mythical figure who adored the spotlight. Gehrig was more reserved, quiet, and shy. Yet, despite their different personalities, they became friends, in no small part because they shared many similarities as well. Both were the descendants of German

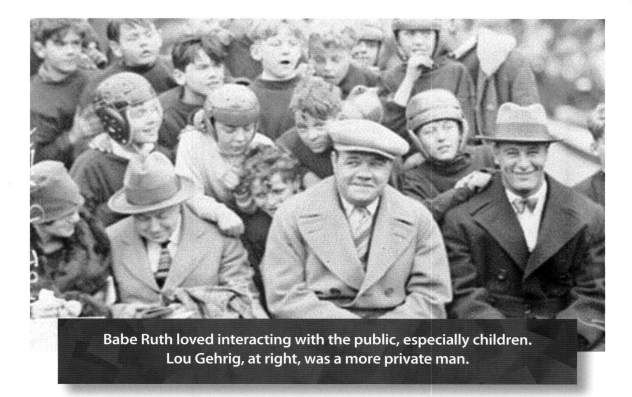

Babe Ruth loved interacting with the public, especially children. Lou Gehrig, at right, was a more private man.

immigrants. Gehrig's parents both arrived in America as young adults before meeting and marrying each other in New York City, and Ruth's grandparents were from Germany. Both players grew up poor in large, East Coast cities, Ruth in Baltimore and Gehrig in New York City. When Gehrig joined Ruth as a player on the New York Yankees, they became part of what many consider the greatest baseball team in history. They batted one after the other, Ruth at the #3 spot in the order and Gehrig at #4. This dangerous Yankees lineup was dubbed "Murderers' Row." In addition to winning championships as teammates, the pair traveled around the country together, barnstorming for extra money in the offseason before heading down south together for spring training.

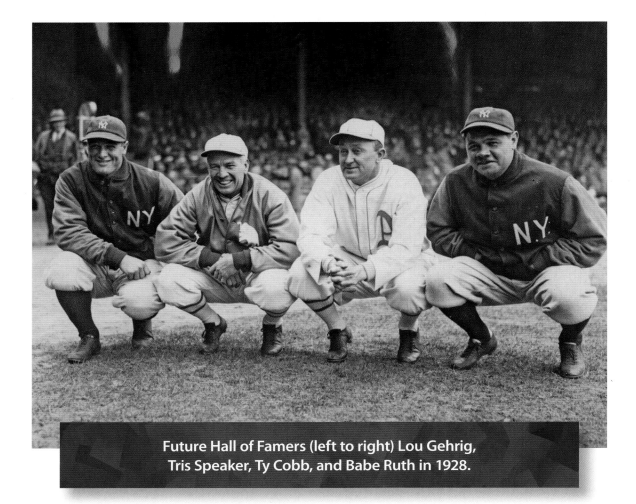

Future Hall of Famers (left to right) Lou Gehrig,
Tris Speaker, Ty Cobb, and Babe Ruth in 1928.

Later in their careers, the pair fell out. They feuded with one another, their friendship at an end, until one player suffered a humiliating retirement and the other faced a tragic end. But before the unhappy ending of their friendship, there were several glorious years during which the pair electrified a city and a nation with their heroics on the field while enjoying a strong friendship off it.

Murderers' Row

The 1926 New York Yankees. Babe Ruth is in the back row, seventh from the left. Lou Gehrig is also in the back row, fifth from the right.

The first six batters in the 1927 New York Yankees lineup were Earle Combs, Mark Koenig, Babe Ruth, Lou Gehrig, Bob Meusel, and Tony Lazzeri. The six were such dangerous hitters that they were nicknamed "Murderer's Row" by the press. There is debate as to whether the name Murderers' Row refers to a stretch of prison cells in New York's notorious Tombs prison or to the dangerous Otter's Alley in lower Manhattan, infamous for its crime.

George Herman Ruth, Jr., shown here at the age of three, was born at 216 Emory Street in Baltimore (top). His childhood home now serves as the Babe Ruth Birthplace and Museum.

Humble Beginnings

2

George Herman Ruth, Jr., was born in the Pigtown neighborhood of Baltimore, Maryland, on February 6, 1895. His parents, George and Katherine, were the children of German immigrants. Of the couple's eight children, only George and his younger sister Mamie survived into childhood. Their father worked hard to provide for the family and their mother was often sick, which allowed young George to skip school and cause mischief around the neighborhood. His parents were constantly finding their seven-year-old son in some kind of trouble and finally reached a breaking point. In order to provide him with some discipline, they sent George away to live at St. Mary's Industrial School for Boys. An orphanage and school on the outskirts of the city, St. Mary's was run by Catholic monks. Later in life, George remembered, "It was at St. Mary's that I met and learned to love the greatest man I've ever known. His name was Brother Matthias. He was the father I needed. He taught me to read and write—and he taught me the difference between right and wrong."[1] The monk also taught young George baseball.

Over the next 12 years, George developed discipline as well as a deep love of baseball, which was played on two of the school's ballfields. He became so

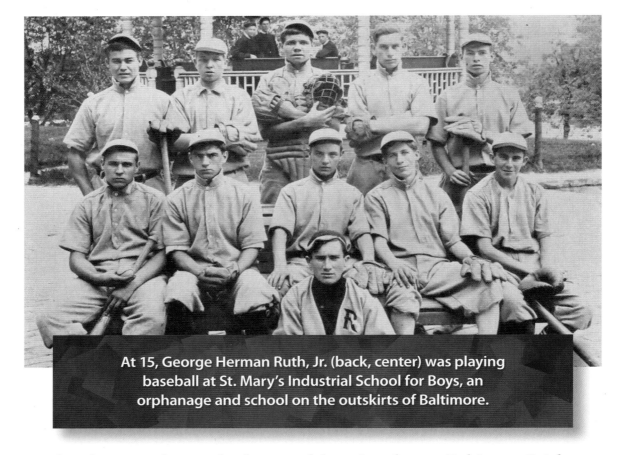

At 15, George Herman Ruth, Jr. (back, center) was playing baseball at St. Mary's Industrial School for Boys, an orphanage and school on the outskirts of Baltimore.

good at the game, he caught the eye of the minor league Baltimore Orioles organization. This team provided players to the major league Boston Red Sox. Since the law said that George was not old enough at 19 to sign on his own, Orioles owner Jack Dunn had to become the young ballplayer's legal guardian. The other Orioles joked that because of this, George was "Dunn's new babe." The nickname Babe stuck, and from then on, George Herman Ruth, Jr., was known as Babe Ruth.

Babe developed quickly and was soon called up to the Boston Red Sox. For the next five years, he was their star pitcher. He would play outfield on the days he wasn't pitching, and contributing runs with his powerful bat. Babe won over 20 games in a season twice as a pitcher for the Red Sox, helping Boston win the championship in 1915, 1916, and 1918. Despite being one of the best left-handed pitchers in baseball, his amazing skill as a hitter soon had him playing every day in the field and pitching less and less often.

After Babe finished his sixth season in Boston, the cash-strapped Red Sox sold Babe to the New York Yankees for the 1920 season. Babe was now a hitter only, his career as a pitcher came to an end. His legendary career with the New York Yankees, however, had just begun.

The Yorkville neighborhood on the Upper East Side of Manhattan was just a few miles from the stadium where Babe Ruth was now playing for the Yankees. It was in Yorkville that on June 19, 1903,

Babe Ruth had a record of 89-46 as a pitcher for the Boston Red Sox. In 1917, he won 24 games.

Henry Louis Gehrig was born. Like Babe, "Lou" was of German descent. His parents, Heinrich and Christina, were immigrants from Germany who had arrived in America just a few years before. The couple had four children, but, as in Babe's family, several of the children died. Lou was the only one of the Gehrig children to survive past infancy. Lou's father had health problems and often couldn't find work, forcing Lou's mother to toil constantly, washing

Lou Gehrig attended Columbia University and played both football and baseball. In 1923, Lou was signed to the New York Yankees.

people's laundry, cleaning houses, and cooking meals to help the family make ends meet. Despite the family's poverty, his mother made sure he always had enough to eat, and Lou grew up strong and athletic. She said, "I don't pretend Lou was born with a silver spoon in his mouth, but he never left the table hungry."[2]

His mother encouraged Lou to seek a good education. In 1921, he received a football scholarship to attend Columbia University in the City of New York, where he would also study to become an engineer. He played fullback during Columbia's 1922 football season, but also made the baseball team, where he played first base and pitched. During one game, "Columbia Lou" struck out 17 batters![3] However, it wasn't his pitching that impressed a New York Yankees scout. It was Lou's hitting. In 1923, the scout signed Lou to a professional baseball contract that came with a signing bonus of $1,500, a great sum of money in those days. Lou and his parents, who were both sick when the contract was signed, would never again want for money.

The House That Ruth Built

Lou Gehrig grew up with a love of baseball. He would seek out baseball games played by older boys in the neighborhood. Sometimes, he'd be able to save up the 25-cent admission to watch his beloved New York Giants play at the Polo Grounds baseball stadium. Later, Gehrig would write, "Back in the days when a quarter was a fortune and we had to save up weeks to get the price of a bleachers seat, the Giants were our favorite."[4] The

Yankee Stadium, seen here in 1923, the year the team moved from the Polo Grounds and into their new $2.4 million home.

Yankees shared the Polo Grounds with the Giants, but in 1922, owner Jacob Ruppert decided to use $2.4 million of his own money to build a beautiful stadium in the Bronx. The Yankees' first game in the stadium when it opened in 1923 was against Babe Ruth's old team, the Boston Red Sox. Ruth hit a 3-run home run as the Yankees won 4-1. Ruth liked the new stadium, saying "Some ballyard, huh?"[5] A sportswriter dubbed Yankee Stadium "The House That Ruth Built" in honor of the slugger. The New York Yankees would win the World Series that year in their new stadium. They would play there for the next 85 years, until the Yankees moved to a new stadium in 2009.

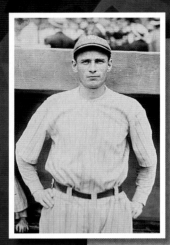

Wally Pipp (inset) was the Yankees longtime first baseman who was replaced in the line-up by the young Lou Gehrig (main photo). While legend says Pipp lost his position to Gehrig because he sat out a game with a headache, the more likely reason was that manager Miller Huggins wanted to shake up his aging lineup by giving younger players a chance.

Teammates and Friends

In June of 1923, Babe Ruth was in the clubhouse at Yankee Stadium when he was approached by trainer Doc Woods. The trainer pointed at a strapping but nervous 19-year-old. "Babe, I want you to meet Lou Gehrig from Columbia," he said, to which Ruth replied, "Hiya, keed."[1] Gehrig, who was already a big fan of Ruth's, was there for his first practice in a Yankees uniform, but he had forgotten to bring a bat. When it came time for batting practice, he picked up a bat that was leaning against the cage, not knowing it belonged to Babe Ruth himself. After a few swings with the bat, Gehrig hammered a home run deep into the bleachers of Yankee Stadium.

At the time, Ruth was in his fourth season with the Yankees, and while he was hitting home runs at a record pace, the Yankees still lost back-to-back World Series. Some people blamed these losses on Ruth's infamous partying lifestyle off the field. There was a great deal of pressure on Ruth in the 1923 season to bring the Yankees a World Series title, and the new rookie who had just homered with Ruth's bat would soon help them do it.

In 1925, Gehrig was put full-time into the Yankees lineup. Over the next 13 seasons, he would play a record 2,130 consecutive games, earning him the

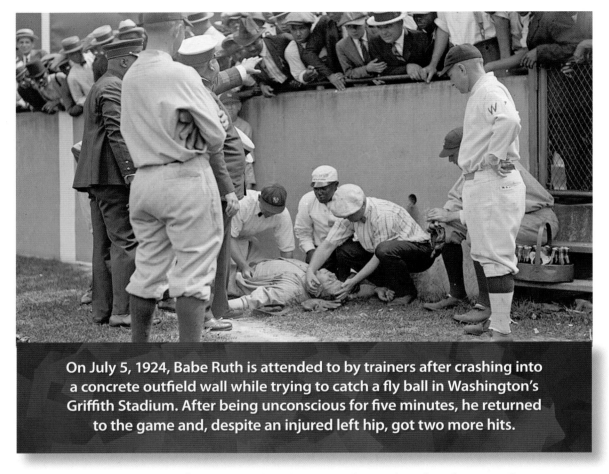

On July 5, 1924, Babe Ruth is attended to by trainers after crashing into a concrete outfield wall while trying to catch a fly ball in Washington's Griffith Stadium. After being unconscious for five minutes, he returned to the game and, despite an injured left hip, got two more hits.

nickname "Iron Horse." Ruth and Gehrig made each other better players. Pitchers would no longer pitch around Ruth and walk him because Gehrig batted right behind him and could drive him in for a run. As Ruth said, "Pitchers began pitching to me because if they passed me they still had Lou to contend with."[2]

In addition to making each other better on the field, Ruth and Gehrig became friends as well. Ruth took the younger player under his wing and taught him about life in the big leagues. Early on, Gehrig was like a little brother to Ruth, listening to his advice on subjects like dealing with reporters. Ruth told him, "You've got to be careful who you talk to and what you say. You've got to be careful about some of these birds."[3]

Gehrig appreciated Ruth's advice. As he once said, "Ruth taught me how to act while on parade. We'd have been to jail more than once if Ruth didn't know how to talk to traffic cops."[4]

By the middle of the 1920s, Gehrig and Ruth were becoming famous, a fearsome one-two punch. During the 1927 season, they combined to hit 107 home runs, more than the total for

Lou Gehrig and Babe Ruth stand together outside a train car in Chicago in 1927.

every other team in baseball except one. The Yankees beat the Pittsburgh Pirates that year four games to none to win the World Series. Since the rules at the time said a player could only win the award once, Babe Ruth did not get the League Award for the most valuable player, despite his record-setting 60 home runs. His teammate Lou Gehrig, however, did take home the prize. The 1927 New York Yankees are often called the best baseball team ever.

During the early years of Gehrig's baseball career, he was always playing in the shadow of larger-than-life Yankees legends. It didn't bother him,

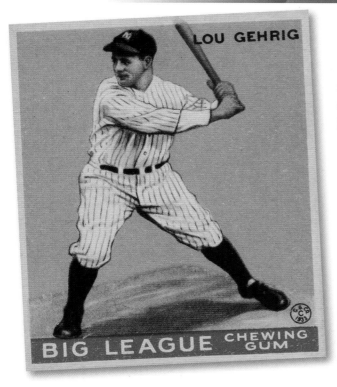

LOU GEHRIG

BIG LEAGUE CHEWING GUM

By 1933, Lou Gehrig had become a star and was escaping the shadow of his more famous teammate Babe Ruth.

though. "It's a pretty big shadow. It gives me lots of room to spread myself," he said.[5]

In 1928, the year after Ruth and Gehrig led the Yankees to their World Series win, Gehrig bought a nice house for himself and his parents in New Rochelle, about 13 miles north of Yankee Stadium. Ruth was often a guest of the Gehrigs. For Ruth, who mostly grew up without a family, being a part of the Gehrigs' home was a treat. Lou's mom, Christina, loved to cook, and Ruth loved to eat, so they got along famously. "It was one of the rare tastes of home life I ever had," Ruth remembered.[6] Christina, who spoke little English, conversed with the Babe in German. She loved to hear about his travels and adventures. She said his given name, George, with a German accent so that it came out as "Judge." When Ruth gave the family a dog for Christmas, Christina named their new pet Judge in Ruth's honor.[7]

Ruth and Gehrig would go fishing together, enjoyed playing cards, golfing, and eating out. The friends even spent large parts of the offseason together, barnstorming across the country to bring big-city baseball to places in the United States that didn't have teams. It wasn't until 1958 that there was even a major league team west of St. Louis, Missouri.

Lou Gehrig and Babe Ruth pose for a photo with famed Hollywood actress Marion Davies at a Chicago railway station.

Barnstorming was a great way for baseball fans with no local major league team to see their heroes in person. It was also a great way for baseball players to make extra money once the regular season was over. Barnstorming trips could have a kind of carnival atmosphere, with vaudeville performances, dancing girls, clowns, and live music.

Lou Gehrig slides headfirst into home plate to score as Washington catcher Hank Severeid awaits the throw.

In 1927, after sweeping the Pittsburgh Pirates in the World Series, Ruth and Gehrig hit the road for a barnstorming tour called "The Symphony of Swat." The pair traveled across the United States that fall. For Gehrig, it was the first time he had been west of the Mississippi River. Ruth led a team called the Bustin' Babes, who wore black shirts and white caps, while Gehrig captained the Larrupin' Lous in white shirts and

In 1927, Babe Ruth and Lou Gehrig played an exhibition game at the United State Military Academy in West Point, New York.

Babe Ruth returned to Providence, Rhode Island, to barnstorm in 1927, having played there for the Providence Grays in 1914. He is shown here in the Grays' team photo in the back row, fifth from the left.

black caps. (Larruping is a word not used much anymore. It means "to thrash" or "to smack.") Before the games, the pair would engage in a very popular home-run hitting contest. On the trips, Gehrig and Ruth would visit orphanages, give speeches, shake hands with local politicians, and play in games against everyone from local amateurs to other major leaguers.

One of their first barnstorming games in 1927 was in Providence, Rhode Island. An ad in the *Providence Journal* advertised the spectacle, saying, "Babe Ruth, King of Swat, and Lou Gehrig, Fence Buster, Will Positively Appear."[8] Thousands of fans showed up. Gehrig and Ruth signed countless autographs for the excited fans. They even took turns on the pitcher's mound!

In the seventh inning of the game in Providence, Gehrig homered off Ruth, sending a monster blast over the center field wall. To get revenge, Ruth

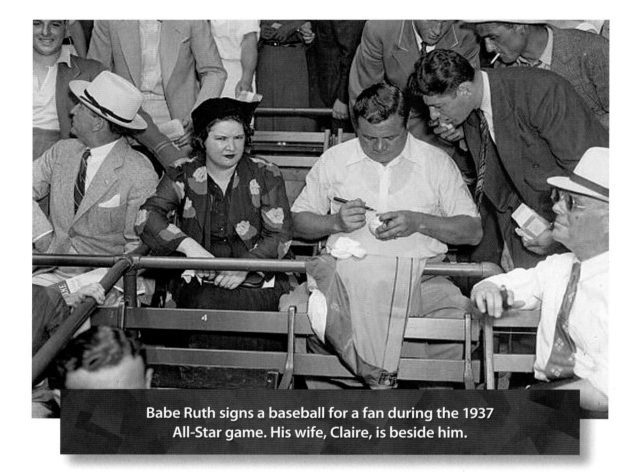

Babe Ruth signs a baseball for a fan during the 1937
All-Star game. His wife, Claire, is beside him.

came to bat in the eighth inning, even though it wasn't his turn. Despite striking out, Ruth refused to leave the batter's box—to the delight of the crowd. After over 20 pitches, the supply of baseballs ran out. A ball autographed by both Gehrig and Ruth was found in someone's pocket. Gehrig pitched that ball and Ruth hit it for a two-run single. The game was called because there were no more balls, Ruth was called out for batting out of order, and Gehrig's team won the game.

Teen Strikes Out Legends

During a barnstorming game in the spring of 1931, Ruth and Gehrig were involved in one of the most remarkable events in baseball history. While traveling from spring training back up to New York, the Yankees stopped to play two exhibition games against the Chattanooga Lookouts, a minor league team in Tennessee. Batting back to back, Ruth and Gehrig were, to the amazement of the 4,000 fans gathered for the game, struck out by a 17-year-old left-handed pitcher named Jackie Mitchell. What was truly amazing was that Jackie was a girl. The teenager from Memphis had been taught to pitch by her neighbor, future Hall of Fame pitcher Charles Arthur "Dazzy" Vance. Jackie and her sinking curveball were so good that she was signed by the Lookouts' president Joe Engel. Always a showman who tried to bring in the crowds with wild stunts, Engel likely made Jackie Mitchell the first woman to sign a pro baseball contract.

A pitcher from the 1913 New York Female Giants. Women have been playing baseball for over a century.

Just weeks after signing, Jackie took the mound to face the mighty Babe Ruth. Ruth took the first pitch for a ball, and then swung and missed at the next two. He didn't swing at Jackie's last pitch and it was called for strike three. Disgusted, or pretending to be, Ruth threw his bat and stalked back to the dugout. Gehrig followed and Jackie struck him out on three straight pitches.

There is controversy to this day as to whether the strikeouts were real or staged. Did Ruth and Gehrig strike out on purpose as part of a show? The two never admitted they faked their strikeouts. As Baseball Hall of Fame research director Tim Wiles said, "Even hitters as great as Ruth and Gehrig would be reluctant to admit they'd really been struck out by a 17-year-old girl."[9]

Lou Gehrig and Babe Ruth pose for a photo with fan Dick Mayes during training camp in St. Petersburg in 1934, the year the friendship between the two players was finally broken.

Falling Out

Gehrig never was the adored, larger-than-life character Babe Ruth was. Ruth was never the health-conscious, modest gentleman Gehrig was. As Ruth once said, "Lou was different than all the others. . . . I could never have been Lou and Lou never could have been me."[1] But together, they made the New York Yankees legendary as they competed for home run and batting titles. Gehrig was emerging from Ruth's shadow and was on the road to becoming a legend himself. Perhaps this contributed to the break in their friendship that was to come. Despite putting up batting numbers similar to Ruth's, Gehrig was being paid about one third as much as Ruth's $80,000 salary.[2]

In the early 1930s, Ruth's 12-year-old daughter Dorothy, adopted during his first marriage, showed up for an overnight visit at the Gehrigs' house. She was dressed like a tomboy as she packed her own clothes while her mother was out of town. Lou's mother, Christina Gehrig, however, was shocked by the way Dorothy was dressed and commented how it was shameful the way Babe's wife, Claire, allowed it. She apparently said that Claire's older daughter Julia "goes to ball games in silks and satins, and poor little Dorothy has nothing but rags to wear."[3]

Babe Ruth and his wife, Claire, (right) board the *RMS Empress of Japan* for a barnstorming trip in October 1934.

When word got back to Claire about what Lou's mother had said, she was very angry. She went to Babe, crying, and told him to "tell Lou to muzzle his mother."[4] Babe, in turn, confronted Lou in the clubhouse, telling him to tell his mother to "mind her own . . . business."[5] Gehrig replied, "You can't talk about my mother that way."[6] Gehrig was very defensive about his mother, whom he adored, and would hear no criticism of her. Ruth felt Gehrig's mother was sticking her nose in where it didn't belong, offending his wife and daughter. He recalled, "Where did she get off saying that about how Claire looked after and dressed the girls?"[7]

The day after their argument in the clubhouse, Ruth reportedly sent Gehrig a note, saying, "Never speak to me again off the field."[8]

The feud was made worse when Ruth talked to a reporter about Gehrig's string of consecutive games. Ruth thought playing without an occasional day off was a bad idea. "This Iron Horse stuff is just a lot of baloney. I think he's making one of the worst mistakes a player can make. He ought to learn to sit on the bench and rest. They're not going to pay off on how many games he's played in a row."[9]

Gehrig was very proud of his streak—a streak that would reach an amazing 2,130 straight games. (That record would last for 56 years, when Cal Ripken, Jr., of the Baltimore Orioles, broke it on September 6, 1995.) To hear his former friend badmouth his achievement pushed Gehrig further from Babe.

By the 1934 season, Ruth knew his career as a player was winding down. He had hoped to become the Yankees manager. Gehrig didn't really think this was a good idea and didn't support Ruth's plan. This disagreement did not help

Lou Gehrig's playing streak got him the nickname "The Iron Horse."

make things any better between the two former friends.

During a 1934 barnstorming trip to Japan, the New York Yankees traded Ruth to the Boston Braves. The trade was finalized in 1935. Gehrig and Ruth, who were no longer friends, were now no longer teammates.

While Babe Ruth was barnstorming in Yokohama, Japan, in 1934, the New York Yankees traded him to the Boston Braves.

Trouble at Sea

Babe Ruth tried to make amends with Lou Gehrig on a 1934 offseason barnstorming trip to Japan aboard the *RMS Empress of Japan*. The team of American League all-stars was sailing out of Vancouver, Canada. Gehrig was worried about having enough money for the trip. As one reporter wrote at the time, "Lou never could forget he was a poor boy once and always worried that he was going to lose his money."[10] Despite their feud, Ruth advanced Gehrig $5,000. Gehrig would later be paid for the barnstorming voyage. Ruth said, "When the trip is over and you get your $5,000, you can pay me."[11]

Babe Ruth met with Japan's Princess Kaya Toshiko and Prince Kaya Tsunenori during his 1934 barnstorming trip.

But the trip by sea ended up dividing the two baseball stars further. Lou's wife, Eleanor, met Babe's wife, Claire, while strolling the ship's deck. Claire invited Eleanor to the Ruths' stateroom for "an empire of caviar and champagne."[12] Lou was unable to find his wife and frantically searched the ship for two hours. He thought perhaps she had fallen overboard! He finally found his tipsy spouse in the Ruths' stateroom. Eleanor remembered, "I stepped into their little world: the resplendent Babe, sitting like a Buddha figure, cross-legged and surrounded by an empire of caviar and champagne. It was an extravagant picnic, especially since I'd never been able to get my fill of caviar, and suddenly I was looking up at mounds of it. So I was 'missing' for two hours. . . . The one place that Lou had never thought to check out was Babe Ruth's cabin."[13] Once he discovered where she was, Lou refused to speak to Eleanor as he took her from the room. Later, Babe came by Lou's room for a "Let's Be Pals"[14] hug, but Lou wanted nothing to do with it.

As Babe Ruth's playing days came to a close in Boston,
Lou Gehrig took over leadership of the New York Yankees
until his career was cut short by a terrible illness.

The Sultan of Swat and the Luckiest Man

Now with the Boston Braves, Ruth knew his playing days were numbered. He was 40 years old and was making more and more mistakes on the field. On May 25, 1935, despite his declining fitness, he went 4-for-4 against the Pittsburgh Pirates, hitting three home runs and batting in six runs. His last home run of the day is said to have bounced off the roof of a home outside the stadium. After sitting back down on the bench following the blast, he said, "Boy, that last one felt good."[1] That was the 714th home run of his career—and his last. Just a few days later, injured and tired, Babe Ruth retired from baseball.

For Lou Gehrig and the Yankees, the game went on. A Canadian player named George Selkirk had replaced Ruth in right field. The Yankees, without Ruth, would go on to win the World Series in 1936, 1937, and 1938. They had their eyes on a fourth straight World Series title in 1939. Gehrig 's powerful hitting, however, had begun to drop off. In the 1938 season, his batting average dropped below .300 for the first time since 1925. Sports reporters noticed that he looked slower running the bases and that playing the game appeared to require more effort. Balls that

Before his diagnosis, Gehrig planned to become a stockbroker after his retirement from baseball.

were once hit for mighty home runs were now routine fly balls caught by the outfielders.

This wasn't just a gradual decline in skills due to age. Something was terribly wrong.

On May 2, 1939, fans were taking their seats to see their Detroit Tigers host the New York Yankees. A message boomed over the stadium's speakers: "Ladies and gentlemen, Lou Gehrig's consecutive streak of 2,130 games played has ended." Gehrig, discouraged by his recent play, had asked to be taken out of the lineup.

There was worse news to come. Gehrig had been diagnosed with amyotrophic lateral sclerosis (ALS), a rare and serious disease that causes the patient to lose the voluntary use of muscles. Over time, walking, swallowing, and then breathing would become impossible. Gehrig would be unlikely to survive more than a few years. ALS soon became known as Lou Gehrig's disease.

On July 4, 1939, 62,000 fans packed Yankee Stadium, joined by many of Gehrig's former teammates, for Lou Gehrig Appreciation Day. Many wondered whether Babe Ruth would show up for the event, since he and Lou had not spoken for years.

Not only did Babe show up wearing a white suit, but he also spoke to the crowd, remembering the glory years of his time with Gehrig and the Yankees: "In 1927, Lou was with us, and I say that was the best ballclub the Yankees ever had."[2] Ruth went on to quip about how Gehrig had time

Despite the long-standing feud between the two, Babe Ruth showed up for Lou Gehrig Appreciation Day at Yankee Stadium. He hugged his ailing former teammate and made a speech to the crowd.

(Left to right) Hall of Famers Jimmie Foxx, Babe Ruth,
Lou Gehrig, and Al Simmons pose for a picture in 1929.

now that he wasn't playing to go catch as many fish as he could. Perhaps Ruth was remembering how he and Gehrig used to go fishing together when they were still friends.

Finally, it was Gehrig's turn to speak. Reluctantly, he approached the microphone and gave one of the most famous speeches in sports history. He began, "For the past two weeks you have been reading about the bad break. Yet today I consider myself the luckiest man on the face of the earth."[3] He went on to thank the fans, his teammates, the Yankees organization, and his family. When he spoke the final words—"So I close in saying that I might have been given a bad break, but I've got an awful lot to live for. Thank you."[4]—everyone in the stadium, including Ruth, was in tears. The crowd applauded for two solid minutes as a band played a German folk song called "You Are Always in My Heart." Ruth walked up to his former friend, extended his hand, then folded Gehrig into a big bear hug. He spoke to Gehrig for the first time in five years, saying, "C'mon, kid. . . . C'mon, kid, buck up now. We are all with you."[5]

The jerseys of Babe Ruth and Lou Gehrig are enshrined together in the Yankee Museum at Yankee Stadium.

Lou Gehrig died on June 2, 1941, at his home at 5204 Delafield Avenue in the Riverdale neighborhood of the Bronx.

Cameras flashed to capture the hug, and a reporter with the *New York Telegram* wrote, "The old king and the crown prince had become reconciled at last."[6]

Lou Gehrig died peacefully at home less than two years later. Babe Ruth paid his respects at the funeral in New York City, tears in his eyes.

The Yankees teammates are enshrined together in the Baseball Hall of Fame in Cooperstown, New York. Lou and Babe will forever be remembered as part of what many consider the greatest team in baseball history.

Many years later, before his untimely death of throat cancer at the age of 53, Babe remembered his one-time friend: "Lou was one of a kind. He was the best friend a fella could have. I wish I could have told him that. I wish I could have told him a lot of things. I loved him."[7]

Lou Gehrig's "Luckiest Man" Speech

"Fans, for the past two weeks you have been reading about the bad break I got. Yet today I consider myself the luckiest man on the face of the earth. I have been in ballparks for seventeen years and have never received anything but kindness and encouragement from you fans.

Lou Gehrig

Look at these grand men. Which of you wouldn't consider it the highlight of his career just to associate with them for even one day? Sure, I'm lucky. Who wouldn't consider it an honor to have known Jacob Ruppert? Also, the builder of baseball's greatest empire, Ed Barrow? To have spent six years with that wonderful little fellow, Miller Huggins? Then to have spent the next nine years with that outstanding leader, that smart student of psychology, the best manager in baseball today, Joe McCarthy? Sure, I'm lucky.

When the New York Giants, a team you would give your right arm to beat, and vice versa, sends you a gift—that's something. When everybody down to the groundskeepers and those boys in white coats remember you with trophies—that's something. When you have a wonderful mother-in-law who takes sides with you in squabbles with her own daughter—that's something. When you have a father and a mother who work all their lives so that you can have an education and build your body—it's a blessing. When you have a wife who has been a tower of strength and shown more courage than you dreamed existed—that's the finest I know.

So I close in saying that I might have been given a bad break, but I've got an awful lot to live for. Thank you."[8]

1895	George Herman "Babe" Ruth is born in Baltimore, Maryland, on February 6.
1902	George's parents send him to live at St. Mary's Industrial School, a school for troublemakers.
1903	Henry Louis "Lou" Gehrig is born on June 19 in Yorkville, New York.
1904	George becomes a permanent resident of St. Mary's Industrial School. He begins playing baseball there.
1914	Ruth is signed to the minor league ball club for the Boston Red Sox, where he is called Babe Ruth. On July 11, he makes his major league debut at Fenway Park in Boston. He and the Red Sox will win the World Series in 1915, 1916, and 1918.
1920	The Red Sox sell Babe Ruth to the New York Yankees.
1921	Gehrig attends New York's Columbia University on a football scholarship.
1922	Gehrig joins Columbia's baseball team.
1923	Gehrig leaves Columbia University to play for the New York Yankees. Ruth wins 23 games with 9 shutouts. The Yankees win the World Series. They will win again in 1927, 1928, and 1932.
1934	Ruth and Gehrig argue. On July 11, Ruth hits his 700th home run.
1935	Ruth is officially traded to the Boston Braves and retires from baseball after playing for a partial season.
1936	Babe Ruth is inducted into the National Baseball Hall of Fame.
1939	Gehrig's health declines. After playing in 2,130 consecutive games, he stops playing baseball. He is diagnosed with amyotrophic lateral sclerosis (ALS). He is inducted to the National Baseball Hall of Fame.

1941   Gehrig dies on June 2.

1948   On August 16, Ruth dies of cancer.

Career Statistics

Name	Batting Avg.	Home Runs	Hits	RBI	Pitching W/L
Babe Ruth	.342	714	2,873	2,213	94-46
Lou Gehrig	.340	493	2,721	1,995	N/A

Babe Ruth played himself in the movie *The Pride of the Yankees*, the story of the life of his former friend and teammate Lou Gehrig, played by actor Gary Cooper (left).

Chapter 2. Humble Beginnings

1. Alan Wood, *Babe Ruth.* Society for American Baseball Research, n.d.,
2. Jonathan Eig. *Luckiest Man: The Life and Death of Lou Gehrig* (New York: Simon & Schuster, 2005), p. 11.
3. "Lou Gehrig Biography," *Biography.com*, April 27, 2017.
4. Eig, p 14.
5. Hermann, Mark. The Babe called it: "Some ballyard, huh?" *Newsday*, June 13, 2008..

Chapter 3. Teammates and Friends

1. Tony Castro, *Gehrig & the Babe: The Friendship and the Feud* (Chicago: Triumph Books, 2018), p. 15.
2. Castro, prologue.
3. Jane Leavy, *The Big Fella* (New York: HarperCollins, 2018), p. 122.
4. Ibid., p. 123.
5. Lou Gehrig official website. Lou Gehrig biography. https://www.lougehrig.com/biography/
6. Steven Goldman, "75 Years Later, Babe Ruth's Hug Means Almost as Much as Lou Gehrig's Speech." *SBNATION,* July 8, 2014.
7. Ibid.
8. Leavy, p. 14.
9. Tony Horwitz. "The Woman Who (Maybe) Struck Out Babe Ruth and Lou Gehrig." *Smithsonian Magazine*, July 2013.

Chapter 4. Falling Out

1. Tony Castro, *Gehrig & the Babe: The Friendship and the Feud* (Chicago: Triumph Books, 2018), p. xviii.
2. Ibid., p. 205.

3. Tony Castro, *Gehrig & the Babe: The Friendship and the Feud* (Chicago: Triumph Books, 2018), pp. 202–3.

4. Billy Heller, "Babe Ruth and Lou Gehrig Were Torn Apart by Women," *The New York Post*, March 31, 2018.

5. Castro, p. 203.

6. Jane Leavy, *The Big Fella* (New York: HarperCollins, 2018), p. 378.

7. Castro, p. 203.

8. Steven Goldman, "75 Years Later, Babe Ruth's Hug Means Almost as Much as Lou Gehrig's Speech." *SBNATION*, July 8, 2014.

9. Ray Robinson. "Ruth and Gehrig: Forced Smiles," *The New York Times*, June 2, 1991.

10. Leavy, p. 413.

11. Ibid.

12. Ibid.

13. Steven Goldman.

14. Leavy, p. 414.

Chapter 5. The Sultan of Swat and the Luckiest Man

1. Jane Leavy, *The Big Fella* (New York: HarperCollins, 2018), p. 417.

2. Tony Castro, *Gehrig & the Babe: The Friendship and the Feud* (Chicago: Triumph Books, 2018), p. 239.

3. National Baseball Hall of Fame: "Luckiest Man."

4. Ibid.

5. Castro, p. 242.

6. Ibid.

7. Castro, p. xxiv.

8. National Baseball Hall of Fame: "Luckiest Man."

Books

Bryant, Howard. *Legends: The Best Players, Games, and Teams in Baseball: World Series Heroics! Greatest Homerun Hitters! Classic Rivalries! And Much, Much More!* (New York: Penguin, 2015).

Christopher, Matt. *Great Americans in Sports: Babe Ruth* (New York: Little, Brown and Co., 2015).

Terrell, Brandon. *Calling His Shot: Babe Ruth's Legendary Home Run.* (North Mankato, MN: Capstone Press, 2019).

Works Consulted

Babe Ruth (Official Website): http://www.baberuth.com.

Baseball-Almanac.com: "1928 World Series." http://www.baseball-almanac.com/ws/yr1928ws.shtml

Baseball-Reference.com: "1928 World Series Game 4, Yankees at Cardinals, October 9." https://www.baseball-reference.com/boxes/SLN/SLN192810090.shtml

Biography.com: "Lou Gehrig Biography." April 27, 2017. https://www.biography.com/people/lou-gehrig-9308266

Castro, Tony. *Gehrig & the Babe: The Friendship and the Feud.* Chicago: Triumph Books, 2018.

Eig, Jonathan. *Luckiest Man: The Life and Death of Lou Gehrig.* New York: Simon & Schuster, 2005.

Goldman, Steven. "75 Years Later, Babe Ruth's Hug Means Almost as Much as Lou Gehrig's Speech," *SBNATION*, July 8, 2014. https://www.sbnation.com/mlb/2014/7/8/5878847/lou-gehrig-babe-ruth-75-anniverary-luckiest-man-speech-forgiveness-history

Heller, Billy. "Babe Ruth and Lou Gehrig Were Torn Apart by Women," *The New York Post*, March 31, 2018. https://nypost.com/2018/03/31/babe-ruth-and-lou-gehrig-were-torn-apart-by-women/

Horwitz, Tony. "The Woman Who (Maybe) Struck Out Babe Ruth and Lou Gehrig." *Smithsonian Magazine*, July 2013. https://www.smithsonianmag .com/history/the-woman-who-maybe-struck-out-babe-ruth-and-lou-gehrig-4759182/#cD7vHSGpCY7QQJZ5.99

Leavy, Jane. *The Big Fella*. New York: HarperCollins Publishers, 2018.

Lou Gehrig (Official Website): https://www.lougehrig.com/

National Baseball Hall of Fame: "Luckiest Man." https://baseballhall.org/ discover-more/stories/baseball-history/lou-gehrig-luckiest-man

Robinson, Ray. "Ruth and Gehrig: Forced Smiles." *The New York Times*, June 2, 1991. https://www.nytimes.com/1991/06/02/sports/baseball-ruth-and-gehrig-forced-smiles.html

Stevens, Julia Ruth, and Bill Gilbert. *Babe Ruth: A Daughter's Portrait*. Dallas: Taylor, 1998.

Vargas, Theresa. "A Baseball Mystery: Did a Teenage Girl Really Strike Out Babe Ruth and Lou Gehrig?" *The Washington Post*, April 25, 2017. https:// www.washingtonpost.com/news/retropolis/wp/2017/04/05/a-baseball-mystery-did-a-teenage-girl-really-strike-out-babe-ruth-and-lou-gehrig/

Wood, Alan. "Babe Ruth." *Society for American Baseball Research*. https://sabr .org/bioproj/person/9dcdd01c

On the Internet

Babe Ruth (Official Website): http://www.baberuth.com

Lou Gehrig (Official Website): https://www.lougehrig.com

National Baseball Hall of Fame: https://baseballhall.org

barnstorm—To travel around the country with exhibition teams in the off-season to play games in a carnival-like atmosphere.

batting average (AV-ridj)—A number that shows how good a hitter is by dividing his number of hits by his number of at-bats. For example, if he gets 4 hits divided by 10 at-bats, his batting average is .400

bleachers (BLEE-churs)—Unsheltered benches used for fan seating, often located along the walls or edges of the outfield of a baseball stadium.

contract (KON-trakt)—A legal document signed by a baseball player and a team that agrees on how long a player will play for the team and for how much pay.

dugout (DUG-out)—The sunken area along the baselines of a baseball field where players not currently on the field wait their turn to bat or play defense.

National Baseball Hall of Fame—A museum in Cooperstown, New York, where the players who were voted as having the best careers are honored.

scout (SKOWT)—The employee of a team whose job it is to go out and look for amateur players who are good enough to become professionals.

season (SEE-zun)—The portion of the year during which a sport is played, ending with playoffs and a championship. In professional baseball, the regular season begins in April and ends in September, lasting 162 games per team. Playoff season begins immediately after the regular season.

spring training—In baseball, the preseason practices held in the spring in warmer climates such as Arizona and Florida.

sweep—Winning every game of a series of games against another team, whether it is in a playoff series or during a multi-day string of games.

vaudeville (VAWD-vil)—A type of entertainment that involved short acts such as singers, dancers, comedians, and magicians.

World Series—A best-of-seven series of games between the best baseball teams from the American and National Leagues to determine the season's overall champion.

Lou Gehrig played himself and starred in the 1938 movie *Rawhide*. The western's story concerned a baseball player (Gehrig) who gave up the sports life to be a cattle rancher.